Living a S T A R B U C K S Lifestyle
On a DUNKIN' DONUTS Budget

**A Millennial's Guide to Getting the Most Out of Life
Without Breaking the Bank**

I0465917

Cover image by Arelissa Gonzalez

Special thanks to Kiersten Lynch for her kind assistance.

Introduction

Millennials (broadly defined here as those in their 20s and 30s) want to enjoy the best things in life as much as everyone else. Yet, their earning potential is typically less than those of older generations. According to SmartAsset.com, Millennials make, on average, about $36,000 a year. Those with a college degree will typically earn more. According to consulting firm Korn Ferry, "2018 college grads in the United States will make on average $50,390 annually." Starting salaries vary by field, of course. An accountant or business major earns around $55,000 a year. Database administrators start around $64,000. Electrical engineers begin their careers at about $75,000, and chemical engineers can make around $79,000 at their first job. Doctors and lawyers often start above $100,000. Frequently saddled with high student loan debt, Millennials need to find ways to live large on a small budget.

This guide will show you how to experience luxury at a bargain.

Coffee

It all starts with coffee. According to the National Coffee Association, nearly two-thirds of us have at least one cup of coffee a day. Among Millennials and others, gourmet coffees are popular. As the demand for coffee goes up, so does the price. According to Zagat, we pay $3.28, on average, for a coffee drink (2015); this is up from $3.05 in 2014 and $2.98 in 2013.

A small cup of Starbucks coffee goes for $2.15. A small cup of Dunkin' Donuts coffee goes for $1.59. You could switch to Dunkin' and save more than $200 a year. But, if you want to treat yourself to Starbucks and still save money, there is a way. At Target and other retailers, you can buy a 12 oz. package of Starbucks ground coffee (which will yield 24 servings) for $7.99. It is often on sale for $5.99! Even at the regular price, that's just 33 cents per cup! So, you can enjoy your Starbucks and save more than $600 a year!

Bonus Tips

- Want to add some spice to your beverage--literally? A friend of mine would keep a small jar of ground cinnamon in his drawer at work. He would add a few sprinkles of cinnamon to his cup, in order to give his regular coffee a gourmet touch.

- What is better than cheap? How about free? Another friend samples a free cup of coffee at the "try it before you buy it" wall at the coffee section whenever she visits Bed, Bath & Beyond.
- You can even collect Starbucks Star Rewards from you Starbucks grocery purchase.

A Word about Tea

According to the Tea Association of the USA, "Tea is the most widely consumed beverage in the world next to water, and can be found in almost 80% of all U.S. households."

FoodDive.com states that, "The influential millennial and Gen Z demographic groups are demanding more from tea just like they are from a host of other foods and beverages. They want more premium and super-premium varieties, and their expectations of what tea should be are changing, pushing the market to adapt. Generally, these younger consumers want healthier beverages brewed with high-quality leaves and botanicals, containing no artificial flavors, and often sold in ready-to-drink glass bottles."

Groceries

According to Earnest.com, Millennials' most frequented grocery stores include Costco (34.5% of all grocery store spending), Kroger (20%), and Whole Foods (16%). According to Acosta.com, Millennials are the most likely of any age group to shop for groceries at multiple locations. Yet, price is not their first concern. Millennials want to buy where they feel they can find freshness and convenience.

Trader Joe's is popular among Millennials. According to Anne Bahr Thompson, of the branding firm, Onesixtyfourth, Millennials "love everything about Trader Joe's – or TJ's, as many call it – from its products to its employees to its kitschy store design." Trader Joe's keeps prices low by cutting out the middleman. The majority of the products are store brands so there is no wholesaler. Trader Joe's passes on the savings to the consumer. We also love Trader Joe's for their "no questions asked" return policy. The stores are also generally compact, making it easy to get in and out.

Whole Foods is often thought of as pricey. Many kiddingly refer to it as "whole paycheck." But you can find values at Whole Foods if you shop their 365 brand.
According to Time.com, Whole Foods recently launched 365 stores which feature the Whole Foods private label brand, similar in concept and price to Trader Joe's.

Bonus Tips

- Make a master list of all the items you buy. Then print (on scrap paper) the list before you head out. Cross off the items you don't need and write quantities next to the items you do need.
- Don't go to the supermarket when you are hungry; you'll buy more than if you go when you are full.
- Buy fresh foods rather than pre-packed. You tend to save money and it is usually healthier.

A Word about Eating Clean

Eating well is not a fad or a diet; it is a way of life. An increasing number of people are looking for ways to eat as healthy as possible.

The concept of eating clean is to eat foods that are minimally processed and contain nothing artificial—no artificial colors, no artificial flavors, or artificial preservatives.

Treat yourself to good food—eat clean!

Craft Beers

Millennials love craft beers because they identify with the independent spirit that craft beers exude over the mass-produced brands.

According to a report by Nielsen published by the Brewer's Association, beer drinkers associate the term "craft" with small, independent, companies, small batch productions, and handcrafted brews. Millennials love the quality and variety of craft beers. They want flavor and freshness.

According to Food & Wine, there are more than 5,000 breweries in the United States, more than anywhere else in the world. They identify some of the top craft beers, and name these as their top ten:

- Sierra Nevada Pale Ale
- Sam Adams Boston Lager
- Goose Island Bourbon County Brand Stout
- Allagash White
- The Alchemist Heady Topper
- Anchor Liberty Ale
- Russian River Pliny the Elder
- 3 Floyds Dark Lord
- Victory Prima Pils
- New Albion Ale

Untapped identified the following as their top ten:
- Founders All Day IPA
- Bell's Two Hearted IPA
- Yuengling Traditional Lager
- New Belgium Voodoo Ranger IPA
- New Belgium Fat Tire
- BrewDog Punk IPA

- Dogfish Head 60 Minute IPA
- Cigar City Jai Alai
- Founders Brewing Kentucky Breakfast Stout
- Stone Brewing Stone Ripper

Whichever you choose, drink responsibly.

A Word about Wine

The health benefits of red wine have long been touted. But, not all wines are created equal. Wines from Sardinia have a greater health benefit than most others. People in Sardinia are known for their longevity. The secret may be in the cannonau grapes.

As always, drink responsibly.

Department Stores

Target (the second most popular brand among Millennials) and Walmart (the seventh most popular) are among Millennials' favorite brands (Moosylvania.com). These discount department stores offer value and convenience. So, what about luxury? According to the Washington Post, Target carries certain high-end brands for less. These include Hunter, Missoni, Alexander McQueen, Jean Paul Gaultier, and Jason Wu.

According to Mashable, Walmart recently introduced premium brands through their online Lord & Taylor division. Brands include Calvin Klein, Effy, Karl Lagerfeld Paris, Lucky Brand, Ray-Ban, Steve Madden, Tommy Hilfiger, Vince Camuto, Brooks Brothers, Kenneth Cole New York, and Nautica.

Macy's is well-known for its upscale merchandise. Recently, Macy's introduced several outlets known as Macy's Backstage which feature items at discounts of up to 80% off. Similarly, Nordstrom's has Nordstrom Rack, where you can find top brands at deep discounts.

Amazon.com is not a department store in the traditional sense, but it is a place (albeit virtual) where you can buy just about anything. Millennials love Amazon. And because Amazon often offers the lowest prices for objects, it is a great and convenient source to shop at.

Bonus Tips

- Macy's offers additional savings for their Macy's credit card holders.
- Target gives you an additional 5% off if you use their RedCard.
- Nordstrom has Nordstrom Notes loyalty rewards program.

A Word about Outlets

So what about outlet stores? According to an article in the *Journal of Fashion Marketing and Management: An International Journal*, researchers found "no signficant differences in the quality of apparel sold" in outlets versus department stores. However, they did find that "the department store merchandise was 31 per cent higher in price than the outlet store merchandise."

Luxury Apartments

According to Pew Research, the vast majority of Millennials (88%) live in metro areas. According to Niche.com, the top 10 cities for Millennials are Cambridge, MA, San Francisco, CA, Arlington, VA, Seattle, WA, Washington, DC, Berkeley, CA, Alexandria, VA, and Denver, CO. New York, NY comes in at number eleven. These rankings are "based on the number of millennial residents, job opportunities, and access to bars, restaurants, and affordable housing" (Niche.com).

Financial technology company SmartAsset looked at the number of millennials moving in and out of major US cities. Based on their research, you can add the following cities to your list: Columbia, SC, Sacramento, CA, Jacksonville, FL, Newport News, VA, San Jose, CA, Norfolk, VA, Virginia Beach, VA, Charlotte, NC, Nashville, TN, and Cincinnati, OH.

PennyHoarder has yet another list. This one focuses on affordability and lifestyle. Their top ten are St. Louis, MO, Grand Rapids, MI, Indianapolis, IN, Columbus, OH, Pittsburgh, PA, Colorado Springs, CO, Nashville, TN, Boulder, CO, San Antonio, TX, and New Orleans, LA.

Other lists of top cities for Millennials abound. In a certain sense, the perfect place is a matter of personal preference. To give you a sense of how much luxury apartments go for, RentCafe compiled average prices of high-end apartments in several major cities. They found that a luxury apartment in El Paso, TX goes for just under $1,000 dollars, while a similar place in New York City goes for more than $4,000.

All of these cities (and others) have up and coming neighborhoods or nearby suburbs which offer luxury at a bargain. As an example, at the time of writing, a luxury one-bedroom, one-bath apartment in Fort Lee, NJ (near the George Washington Bridge) was listed at $1,850 a month. This includes a view of the New York skyline, 24-hour doorman, gym, tennis court, two pools, all utilities and one parking space. You can find similar gems in or near the city of your choice.

Bonus Tips

- Give yourself plenty of time to find the right place, but when you do, act quickly.
- If you have excellent credit and a steady job, you may be in a position to negotiate a better rent or better terms on your lease.
- When narrowing your choices, drive by each place during different times of day and night to get a complete picture of what the neighborhood is like.

Cars

Millennials like Ford, Toyota, Chevrolet, and Honda. Among the luxury brands, they prefer BMW.

U.S. News & World Report has compiled a list of luxury vehicles for less than $35,000. Models include the Acura ILX, Infiniti QX30, Audi A3, Buick Envision, Mercedes Benz CLA, BMW X1, Lincoln MKC, and Volvo s60.

Bonus Tip

- Buy a vehicle with 5,000 miles or so. While it is not new, it will be as good as new; but a lot cheaper.
- Always negotiate. Check websites such as KBB.com, CarMax, and Edmunds to see how much you should pay.
- Don't buy the extended warranties.

Car Rentals

Savvy travelers know that if you rent a car at an airport location, you pay a premium. A friend of mine finds a rental location near the airport and takes Uber or Lyft from the airport to the remote location. He saves lots of money this way.

Use a credit card that will provide insurance on auto rentals and avoid paying the rental company's insurance. If you accumulate airline miles, see if you get miles for renting with certain car rental partners. Shop around for the best deals on sites such as Kayak.com.

Bonus Tips

- Don't prepay for gas. Instead, use your cell phone to find a cheap place to fill up just before you get to the rental return center.
- Don't pay for GPS or satellite radio--you can use your phone for these things. Buy a cheap clip and take it with you.
- Think twice whether or not you actually need a rental. Perhaps Uber and public transportation are a better option in some cities. Splurge on a nice restaurant with the money you save.

Airlines

The best way to pay less for first class is to start off with a budget airline.

Southwest Airlines is a favorite among millennials, both as an airline and as a place to work (according to Indeed.com). In fact, according to a recent survey from Morning Consult, Southwest is the favorite airline of most Americans. However, Southwest does not have first class.

Jetblue is a good choice for those seeking "luxury" without paying extra. Jetblue offers the most legroom in economy class. If you want more, go for JetBlue Mint.

If you are **flying** internationally, WiseBread.com recommends that you look into La Compagnie, a tiny airline that flies from Newark to Paris with all first class seats. They also suggest Norwegian Air which offers service to major European cities for less than the better-known competitors.

Look for offers from the airlines which provide as many as 50,000 miles for getting their credit card and meeting a particular spending threshold. Some waive the annual fee for the first year and others have no annual fee. Shop around!

Bonus Tips

- If there is something wrong, complain. If you have a legitimate gripe, respectfully let them know. They may give you an upgrade in order to remedy the situation.
- Always look for nearby airports for departure and landing. You might save a bundle by going to an airport that might be an hour or so from your destination.

- Bid to upgrade. You might win an upgrade for far less than if you had booked it from the get go. Just be sure that you will be okay in economy class if you don't get the upgrade

A Word about Airport Lounges

Sure, airline lounges at the airport can be nice. But, you are not always going to be able to spend your time at a posh lounge. Make your experience at the gate as best as possible. Plan ahead and bring a snack or meal. Bring a tablet to help pass the time. And no one said you have to wait at your own gate (which may be crowed). Move to a nearby gate with fewer people waiting until boarding time.

Hotels

Getting a luxury room at a hotel is always a good thing. Here's a few ways to get more for less at hotels and resorts.

First tip is to always ask for an upgrade. There's no harm in asking! Front desk staff might be particularly receptive if you mention that you are celebrating a special occasion such as an anniversary or a birthday. They might also be receptive to a nice tip handed discreetly.

Using booking websites is a good way to shop around for the best price. Loyalty programs are also worth looking into.

A great way to score a luxury room for less is to stay in the financial district of a city. These rooms are typically high-end accommodations catering to business travelers and often go for less during weekends.

If you want to experience a few minutes of opulence for free, you can always hang out in the lobbies of large, fancy hotels. If you look as though you belong, you will probably go unnoticed.

Disney World

Disney is one of the top 25 favorite brands among Millennials (according to Moosylvania.com). The happiness at the Happiest Place on Earth can sometimes come at a steep price. But you don't have to pay an arm and a (turkey) leg to enjoy the best Disney World has to offer. Mousesavers.com is replete with money-saving tips. The first thing to know is that Disney World has different seasons and prices for resort rooms vary accordingly.

Some of the deepest discounts are available to those who attend conferences hosted at Disney World resorts. Doctors, accountants, educators, and other professionals can attend conferences and pay around $225 for a room that usually goes for hundreds more. Many of these conventions also offer discounted park tickets.

Bonus Tips:

- Don't buy water at the park. Instead, ask for ice water at one of the counter service restaurants. Save that money to splurge on something else.
- Take advantage of the Magical Express which is free transportation to and from the Orlando International Airport.

Cruises

CruiseCritic.com has identified certain cruise lines as appealing to Millennials.

U by Uniworld is cruising reinvented. For starters, it is a river cruise, as opposed to the more common ocean cruises. It also caters specifically to Millennials. As the company states on their website, they see themselves as "a new take on experiential travel, with cruises designed for those with a passion for exploring and a taste for authentic adventures." This is certainly not your typical cruise experience.

Ocean cruise lines that Cruise Critic identifies as a good fit for those in their 20s and 30s include Celebrity, Royal Caribbean, Disney, Norwegian, and others. Of course, it is important to choose an itinerary that fits your interests.

.

Bonus Tips

- Board as early as you are allowed so that you can have lunch on the ship and begin enjoying your vacation right away.
- If you have your picture taken by the photographers on the ship, negotiate a package deal at the end of your cruise. You might get a free memory stick with all your pictures.

Clothing & Shoes

Millennials shop for their clothing and footwear at Express, American Eagle, Old Navy Aeropostale, and Banana Republic, among others. A popular way to save money is the app RetailMeNot.

When shopping for apparel from certain designers such as Michael Kors, Ralph Lauren, or Kate Spade, try outlet stores or factory stores.

Bonus Tips

- Buy and sell on PoshMark and similar sites. Most of us get bored of our clothes after a while. It makes sense to sell it and buy something else for considerably less than original price.
- Wait for items to go on sale. Avoid buying when things first hit the shelves and racks. Stores tend to reduce the price after a couple of weeks or so.
- You can find many top brands at deep discounts at places such as Burlington Coat Factory, Marshalls, or T.J. Maxx.

Jewelry, Watches and Handbags

This is a category where people can spend a great deal of money. As such, it lends itself to a great many scams, including fakes and knockoffs. If bling is your thing, proceed cautiously.

BREAKFAST

MAINS

MASALA OMELET
rolled Indian omelet, tomato, cilantro, green chilies 25

FRIED EGG RANCHEROS
spicy tomato confit, whipped avocado 28

VANILLA WAFFLE
strawberry compote, whipped cream 25

BRIOCHE FRENCH TOAST
cinnamon sugar 25

BUTTERMILK PANCAKES
choice of chocolate chip, blueberry or banana 24

SMOKED SALMON & BAGEL
red onions, capers 20

WELLNESS BREAKFAST

ENERGY
Ancient grains with mushrooms, kale, poached
egg served with our Wellness Juice 34

VITALITY
Homemade high fiber granola with Greek
yogurt served with a jar of Tie Guan Yin
Imperial Tea (single estate oolong tea) 12

BAKERY

VIENNOISERIE 14

BREAKFAST BAGUETTE 9

TOAST OR BAGEL 9

CONTINENTAL BREAKFAST

Choice of coffee, tea, espresso, cappuccino or latte.
Choice of juice or small fresh fruit salad. 31

Select of one of the following:

VIENNOISERIE

ENGLISH MUFFINS, TOAST OR BREAD SELECTION

SLICED MELON & PAPAYA
with lime

STEEL CUT IRISH OATMEAL, DRY CEREAL

COLD CUTS
French & Virginia ham, prosciutto, mortadella, add 6

AMERICAN BREAKFAST

Choice of coffee, tea, espresso, cappuccino or latte. Choice of juice or small
fresh fruit salad. Choice of breakfast pastry, muffin or toast. 42

Select one of the following:

TWO EGGS ANY STYLE
with sausage or bacon

HAM & CHEESE OMELET
three eggs, French ham, Swiss cheese

EGG WHITE OMELET
spinach, tomatoes, asparagus

EGGS BENEDICT
Canadian bacon or smoked salmon, add

Substitute breakfast pastry, croissant or any two of our side
orders. Add an order of breakfast meat for 8.

SIDES

HALF GRAPEFRUIT 8

MIXED BERRIES 11 / 22
add Greek yogurt or cottage cheese 4

FRUIT SALAD 9 / 18

SLICED MELON & PAPAYA 16

AVOCADO 6

CATSKILLS SMOKED SALMON 23

BREAKFAST MEATS 8
choice of Applewood smoked bacon, Canadian or
turkey bacon, chicken or pork sausage

BEVERAGES

COFFEE, TEA 6

ESPRESSO 8 / 12

FRESH JUICE 9.50

CAPPUCCINO, CAFE CREME 10 / 12

HOT CHOCOLATE 10

WELLNESS JUICE 12
green juice of beets, spinach, green apple, celery,
carrot, red beets, ginger, parsley, orange

MANGO LASSI 5

YOGURT SMOOTHIE 4
mango, strawberry, protein

ELIXA COCONUT WATER 9
organic, unprocessed water

Restaurants

A Recent article in Forbes.com cited the Food Institute's analysis of the United States Department of Agriculture's food expenditure data which states that Millennials spend 44% of their food dollars – or $2,921 annually – on eating out. This outpaces baby boomers who spend 40% of their food dollars on eating out or $2,629 annually.

A great way to treat yourself to a nice restaurant without breaking the bank is to dine during restaurant week. Most large cities and many suburbs have such an event. Typically, you get to enjoy a two-course lunch or a three-course dinner for a fixed price.

Of course, you are not going to do fine dining every night. Chick-fil-a, Chipotle, and Panera are favorites among Millennials. They do not represent "luxury" but are a step-up from fast-food options.

You can also recreate a fine dining experience at home if you take the time to put a little creativity into your meals. A nice table cloth, some candles, soft music...you get the picture.

Bonus Tips

- Alcohol is expensive, so find a great, quality restaurant that is BYOB.
- If possible, split large meals between two people, or order a doggy bag. This way, you have gotten more bang for your buck.
- Pay with a credit card that has generous cash back rewards for eating out.

A Word about Delivery Services

Millennials are more likely than other generations to order food delivery. Food delivery is a multi-billion dollar industry. Each delivery can run you around $10 (especially if you tip the driver). Understandably, some days food delivery is a necessity. But, it is easy to get into a habit of ordering delivery every night. This is not good for your wallet or your waistline.

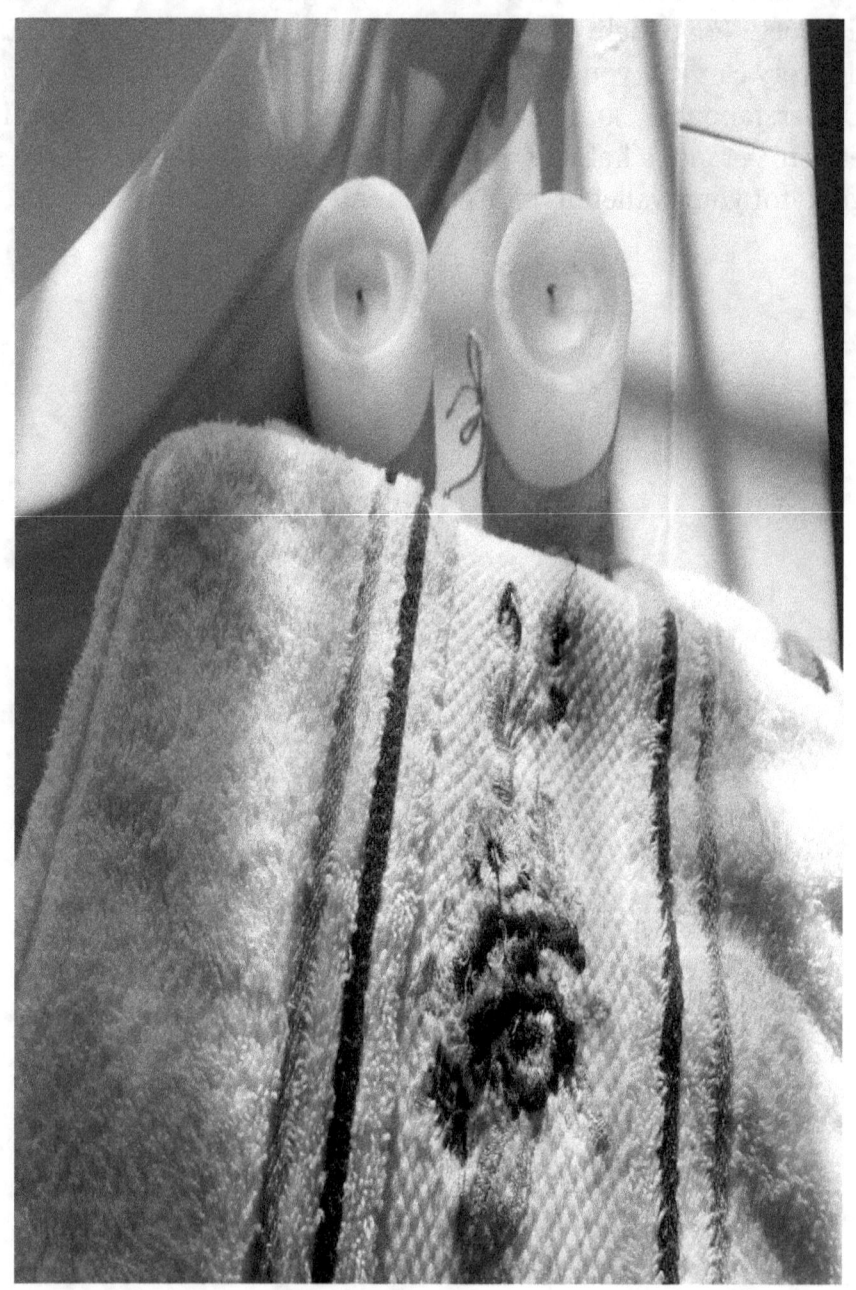

Spas and Massage Services

Like with many other services and products, you can find good deals for spa and massage providers from Groupon or Living Social. What's more, just like there is Restaurant Week, there is also Spa Week. Check out the website SpaWeek.com for details and deals. Massage Envy is a good choice for pampering without a break-the-bank price tag.

Another way to pamper yourself on a budget is to purchase a massager for home. Some of the newer gadgets are economical and provide a great massage.

Saving Money on Little Things = More Money for Luxuries

There are countless ways to save money (and, therefore, have more money for luxuries). Here are some of our favorites.

- Pack a lunch for work/school
- Pack a water bottle
- Shop by "unit price"
- Lower the thermostat
- Use coupons, but only for things you already buy
- Don't go to the supermarket hungry; prepare the list ahead of time
- Get rid of your house phone (landline)
- Use streaming instead of cable or satellite
- Use a "cash back bonus" credit card
- Quit smoking
- Turn off the lights when you leave the room
- Replace light bulbs with high-efficiency bulbs
- Buy non-perishables in bulk
- Make your own cleaning supplies
- Reuse paper towels
- Do your own nails
- Walk or bike, when possible
- Wait for movies to come out On Demand
- Ask for student discounts
- Buy only on sale

Ways to Make Extra Money Also = More Money for Luxuries

You can also explore ways to earn more money. Here are a few suggestions.

- Ask for a raise/get a new job
- Work overtime (if possible)
- Have a garage sale
- Sell unused clothing on Poshmark or similar sites
- Sell unused items on Ebay, etc.
- Babysit or pet sit
- Get paid to tutor
- Drive Uber
- Sell your photos online
- Take online surveys

<u>A Final Note</u>

Ultimately, luxury is a state of mind. It is being happy with what you have (and not sweating what you don't). Take time to reflect on the truly priceless things in life.

www.ingramcontent.com/pod-product-compliance
Lightning Source LLC
Chambersburg PA
CBHW071243220526
45468CB00002B/980